P9-EKR-415

CALGARY PUBLIC LIBRARY

OCT   2016

First published in Belgium and Holland by Clavis Uitgeverij, Hasselt – Amsterdam, 2015
Copyright © 2015, Clavis Uitgeverij

English translation from the Dutch by Clavis Publishing Inc. New York
Copyright © 2016 for the English language edition: Clavis Publishing Inc. New York

Visit us on the web at www.clavisbooks.com

No part of this publication may be reproduced or stored in a retrieval system, or transmitted in any form or by any means, electronic, mechanical, photocopying, recording, or otherwise, without the prior written permission of the publisher, except in the case of brief quotations embodied in critical articles and reviews.
For information regarding permissions, write to Clavis Publishing, info-US@clavisbooks.com

Mack's World of Wonder. All About Forests written and illustrated by Mack
Original title: *Wondere wereld. Het dikke bosboek*
Translated from the Dutch by Clavis Publishing

ISBN 978-1-60537-301-0

This book was printed in June 2016 at Publikum d.o.o., Slavka Rodica 6, Belgrade, Serbia

First Edition
10 9 8 7 6 5 4 3 2 1

Clavis Publishing supports the First Amendment and celebrates the right to read

ALL ABOUT
FORESTS

Mack

Clavis

NEW YORK

THE FOREST

THE FOREST

If you walk into a forest, you can see trees everywhere. Trees, trees and more trees. Some trees are very tall: sometimes as tall as a house! Other trees are very small. If you look up in the forest, you can see hardly any blue sky; nothing but green leaves or needles. The forest is perfect for playing hide-and-seek. You can hide behind the tree trunks, or behind the bushes on the ground.

Many animals live in and among the trees and
bushes of the forest. Deer, squirrels, birds,
rabbits.... Most animals spend their entire lives
in the same forest. The forest is their home.

Which forest dwellers do you see here?

THE TREES

There are different types of forests with different species
of trees. In a deciduous forest, you find only deciduous trees. These are
trees with leaves that change color in the fall and then fall to the ground.
A coniferous forest has trees with needles instead of leaves. They cling
to the tree, even when it gets cold. But beware, those needles are prickly!
Coniferous and deciduous trees live together, in many forests.

conifer

Trees need sunlight to grow. The leaves of a tree make oxygen out of sunlight. That's very nice, because people and animals need oxygen to breathe. Thank you, trees!

deciduous tree

Can you tell the difference between coniferous and deciduous trees?

THE TREES

Besides trees, you also find many bushes and other plants in a forest. What's nice is that every bush and plant has something special to offer. One has beautiful flowers, the other delicious fruit. But you also have plants that sting, like the nettle. Or plants that climb up trees. Even the plants that aren't really beautiful are often very useful. Sometimes medications are made from them, helping you get better when you are sick!

Most forest animals eat only plants. Look!
This bird has already found some delicious fruit,
which he is soon going to enjoy.

Which bush has most berries?

THE FOREST FLOOR

On the forest floor you can see parts of the roots of the trees. They stick their roots in the earth as deep as they can to find food and water. Small plants such as grass and dandelions grow in the soil of the forest. In the summer the yellow dandelions change into fluffy puffballs. If you blow away all the fluff at once, you can make a wish. But don't tell anyone what you wished for! Because then your wish won't come true.

Most of the animals in the forest live on the ground. Bunnies play hide-and-seek there and sometimes you see a squirrel scampering along — if he has had enough of climbing in the trees.

What lives and lies on the forest floor?

THE TREES

DECIDUOUS TREES

Deciduous trees are trees with flat leaves. Each kind of tree has
different leaves. The large leaves of an oak have ruffled edges and
the leaves of the beech are beautifully jagged. The trunks of the different
types of trees look different too. Long and narrow, or shorter and wider,
dark brown or white.... You can identify any deciduous tree immediately
by its trunk and its leaves. The birds in the forest all have their favorite
type of tree to build a nest in!

Leaves of deciduous trees change
color when it gets colder.
Then they fall from the tree.

Which leaf is not from a deciduous tree?

CONIFERS

Conifers do not have big, flat leaves, but thin, hard leaves. They are like needles or spines. That's because conifers used to grow only in cold regions with frost and snow. The needles can withstand the snow. In warm weather, the needles of coniferous trees can sometimes be a little discolored. They don't enjoy the heat. Conifers prefer wintertime. A deciduous tree loses its leaves in winter but not a conifer. Needles are fond of cold.

A conifer is not afraid of a little snow. It simply clings to the needles.

Which leaves come from a conifer?

OLD TREES

Trees can get very old. Older than your father and mother, your grandparents, even older than the oldest tortoises, which are more than two hundred years old! An oak tree, for example, can easily live a thousand years. There are trees that saw Roman soldiers walk past their trunks. Those Romans no longer exist, but the trees are still alive!

Old trees are big, they have gnarled roots and often they have hollow trunks. Rabbits can have fun playing hide-and-seek in them.

Trees grow a little bit thicker every year. They get a new growth ring in their trunk each year so you can easily tell how old the tree is.

Which trunk is from an old tree and which is from a young one?

TREES WITH NUTS

Trees are very large, but they start their lives being very small. As small as a sapling. Or even smaller… as small as a nut. When the nuts fall from the tree and settle into the soil, new trees grow from them. Not from every nut, of course! Then the forest would soon be full! Many nuts are eaten by animals. A single nut that survives will grow into a beautiful big tree.

*Thousands of beech nuts
grow on a single beech tree.*

Which tree has the most nuts under it?

CHESTNUT TREES

The best nuts in the forest are the chestnuts. They grow inside bright green husks hanging from the tree. You'd better not touch that husk, because it has prickly spines. When the chestnut is ripe, the prickly husk pops open automatically. Then the shiny brown chestnut comes out and falls to the ground.

Sweet chestnuts have a soft point and a husk with long, thin spines. Sweet chestnuts are quite tasty.

Horse chestnuts have no point, and have a husk with short, stiff spines. You can't eat horse chestnuts.

Sweet chestnuts

Horse chestnuts

Which chestnuts can you eat?

THE FOREST DWELLERS

THE CLIMBERS

The animals of the forest really feel at home there. With such
tall trees, it is useful to be a good climber. Tree martens
and squirrels are the best climbers. They don't even have to practice.
A squirrel can climb even better than he can walk. On the ground,
he hops a bit, but he can climb up a tree in no time because he has firm,
sharp nails. That's how squirrels can hold on tight to the tree's trunk.

Tree martens hunt small animals.
They jump quickly from tree to tree
after their prey. Squirrels do not have
to run as fast. They love nuts, which grow
high in the trees and don't run away!

Which squirrel is happy with his nuts?

THE PREDATORS

Predators love the forest. They come here to hunt smaller animals, like frogs or mice. But it's not always easy, because little mice can hide really well. That's why the bigger animals think of different tricks to surprise them. Birds attack from the sky, badgers go hunting at night and foxes often hide in the tall grass before they jump out. So little mice always have to be alert!

The black-and-white badger goes hunting at night, when the mouse is a little sleepy. Birds of prey stalk their prey from the sky. Mice have to look up every now and then, or they turn into a tasty meal!

Which mouse is doing a good job of hiding from the birds of prey?

THE FORAGERS

The forest ground is like a restaurant for many animals. They find the tastiest meals here: acorns, chestnuts, mushrooms…. Of course one meal is better than another and the best treats are hidden far beneath the leaves and a layer of dirt. That's why boars, hedgehogs and other foragers have a very good nose. They use it to sniff the ground, looking for food for themselves and their little ones.

Wild boars have such a good nose that they can find the best mushroom in the world: the truffle. People are crazy for them too!

Which hedgehog is a good forager?

Birds need a safe place to build their nests. That is why you find many birds in a forest. They make nests out of branches high up in the trees. Or they look for a hollow tree where they can lay their eggs. When the baby birds hatch from the eggs, the parents fly to and fro with worms, insects and other food. The baby birds grow strong so that they can leave the nest and fly away on their own.

You see lots of different birds in a forest. Robins, titmice, owls…. The bird with the strongest beak is the woodpecker. Woodpeckers can carve a nest from the hardest tree trunk. They don't use any tools — only their beaks!

Do you recognize the woodpecker and the owl?

THE CRAWLERS

A lot of very small animals live in the forest: caterpillars, beetles, worms, bugs, spiders and ants. They often crawl right in front of you, and you don't even notice. But you can't miss an anthill, it is so incredibly big. Many thousands of ants live there. All these ants work together to build their house. One ant carries a branch, another one puts it in the right place, and another helps fight off enemies. Every ant has his own task. Isn't that wonderful?

Sometimes you see a caterpillar hanging from a tree branch. If you stay and watch for a while, you can see how the caterpillar makes a second skin around himself: a cocoon. He stays in there for a while and then... the caterpillar changes into a butterfly! They look like two very different animals, but a caterpillar is really a young butterfly.

Dung beetles eat animal droppings. Isn't that disgusting?

Which ant can lift the heaviest weight?

THE BURROWERS

Not all the animals of the forest sleep in the trees. Some animals
sleep underground. Rabbits, foxes and badgers dig a burrow to live in.
Or they find the burrow of another animal, and then they move in with
the whole family. That's easier, of course. Animals feel safe in the burrow.
It is nice and warm, and shelters them from the rain.

Moles dig long tunnels under the ground where they live. The mole hardly ever sticks his head above the ground!

Which of these animals live in a burrow?

WATER ANIMALS

You can sometimes find water in a forest: a river, a lake or a ditch. You hear croaking, twittering and buzzing sounds around the water. That's because of all the frogs, birds and insects that live there. Ducks are always swimming in the water. Or maybe swans. Swans are very beautiful animals with long necks. But don't get too close to swans with their young, because then they'll get very angry!

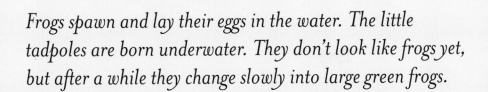

Frogs spawn and lay their eggs in the water. The little
tadpoles are born underwater. They don't look like frogs yet,
but after a while they change slowly into large green frogs.

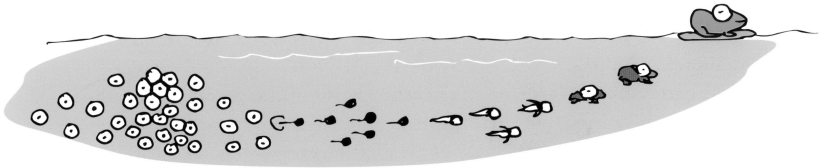

When does the tadpole begin to look like a frog?

HIDE-AND-SEEK ANIMALS

There are many good hiding places in a forest. You can go and stand behind a tree trunk, of course. But some animals are very good at staying invisible all the time. If no one sees them, they won't get eaten. Deer are big animals with enormous antlers. But you won't notice them because of their color. Deer are the real hide-and-seek masters of the forest.

Birds and butterflies often have flashy colors, but some of them you can hardly see!

Which animals are hiding in the bushes?

THE MUSHROOMS

If the forest floor is damp, mushrooms come popping out one by one from the earth. With their graceful stalks and their colorful tops, they look delicious. And sometimes you can eat them too. But be careful, because there are poisonous mushrooms in the forest! You'd better not pick this spotted toadstool, for example. It's beautiful, but as toxic as ten spiders. Don't touch it!

Mushrooms often grow in groups, like this fairy ring. They are all connected in a circle under the ground. That is why they remain so close together!

Which toadstool is poisonous?

SEASONS

SPRING

In spring the trees of the forest grow new leaves. The cold winter is over and small buds appear on the bare branches of deciduous trees. Fresh young leaves grow from them. Hundreds of leaves. It looks like an explosion of green! Flower buds in different colors appear amidst the green on the ground. Butterflies love them! Meanwhile birds build their nests in the trees. Thus the forest comes back to life in spring.

Flowers don't just grow on the ground.
Some flowers grow on tree branches
in spring too. These flowers have
a special name: blossoms.

Which flowers are already in bloom?

SUMMER

The sun feels warmest in summer. But you won't notice the warmth in the forest. The new leaves that appeared in spring grow large in the summer, so the forest is covered in cool shade. Poppies love the sun; they only bloom when it is shining, just like sunflowers. Bees buzz through the forest in summertime. They fly from flower to flower and spread flower seeds everywhere: it's called pollen. Thanks to the bees, new plants, flowers and trees will grow!

In summer, bees fly buzzing from flower to flower.

Which animals do you only see in summer?

FALL

In the fall, the whole forest changes color. It looks as if an artist is walking from tree to tree with a paintbrush dipped in yellow, orange and red paint. The color green disappears from the forest. And eventually the leaves disappear too. One by one, they fall from the branches. Now that winter is coming, the trees can't get enough water from the ground to feed all leaves.

The leaves of the trees aren't the only things falling in the fall; the nuts fall too. Squirrels come running to eat them or to hide them. They collect food to survive the cold winter.

Which leaves do you see in the fall?

WINTER

It's very cold in the forest in winter. Snow can fall from the clouds and the ground freezes. If there's a hard freeze, icicles will cover the branches. Forests might sometimes look like a fairy tale in winter, but the trees actually don't like the snow and cold all that much. In winter, deciduous trees don't grow any leaves, flowers or nuts.... A tree doesn't do much in winter, to be honest. It's just waiting for spring to come.

Conifers do like winter. They stay nice
and green, even when it freezes!

Which trees do you see in winter?

FORESTS AROUND THE WORLD

THE RAINFOREST OF BORNEO

Palm trees and other tropical trees grow in the warmest places in the world. In some places, you can find forests full of them. These forests are called tropical rainforests and jungles. Hundreds of different plants and trees grow on the Asian island of Borneo. Beautiful birds live in the trees, like this hornbill. You can tell where the hornbill got his name, can't you?

Not just birds live in Borneo's rainforest,
but also poisonous frogs and orangutans.
These apes use their hands and their feet
to swing from tree to tree.

Yummy chocolate
is made from
the cacao bean below.

Do you recognize the bananas?

THE SEQUOIA TREES OF CALIFORNIA

Very tall trees grow in California: giant sequoias.
Sequoias are tall pine trees and giant sequoias or redwood trees
are very tall pine trees. The tallest trees in the world! Many giant
redwoods are even taller than a church or an office building.
The needles of redwoods remain green and you'll easily recognize,
their soft, reddish-brown bark.

Sequoias are very tall,
but also very wide!
A hundred children
can easily stand around
the roots of the tree without
touching each other.
Incredible, right?

Which tree is the sequoia?

THE BAMBOO FORESTS OF CHINA

Bamboo is a very strong plant. If you plant bamboo in the garden, it can easily grow through a stone or a thick board. Green leaves grow right at the top of the bamboo plant, but the stem is unusual: it is hollow! The strong bamboo stalks are used to make furniture and musical instruments such as the flute. Bamboo stalks can also grow very high. Just look at this giant bamboo forest in China!

The giant panda loves eating tender bamboo leaves. As a matter of fact, he chews on leaves in China's bamboo forests all day long. The Chinese must be very careful with these forests, because when the bamboo forests disappear, so does the panda!

Which panda is feasting on delicious bamboo?

One of the most unique trees in the world is the baobab. It has a very thick trunk and a small tuft of branches at the top. It looks like the tree is standing upside-down, with its roots growing upwards. The baobab grows mainly in hot, dry areas in Africa. During the rainy season, the baobab tree stores water in its thick trunk. It keeps some for when the weather gets drier. That's a pretty smart tree!

The baobab tree towers over the warm plains of Africa. From here the marabou stork has a nice view of the other animals.

Baobab trees grow in Africa. Which animals also live there?

You might know the smell of eucalyptus. If you have a cold and your nose is completely stopped up, eucalyptus can help you breathe better again. We get that smell from the leaves of the eucalyptus tree. The eucalyptus tree grows mainly in Australia. Koala bears live in eucalyptus trees and almost never come down! Koala bears use their big noses to smell the leaves; if the smell is good, they eat them too.

You can become a little groggy from eating eucalyptus leaves. That's why koala bears are so drowsy and always sleeping in the eucalyptus trees.

Which koala is a little groggy?

THE FLOWER FOREST

In England you find forests that are known not just for their trees, but also for their flowers. In spring, when it gets a bit warmer, bluebells appear everywhere. Not one, or a few clumps, but countless purple flowers. It looks as if the entire forest is covered with a purple carpet! If you take a walk in the woods, you have to be careful, because before you know it, you can trample a beautiful bluebell!

Wild horses and ponies graze in the English moorlands. They keep the grass short and love to eat dandelion leaves.

Which flower has most green leaves for the horse?

The taiga is one of the biggest forested areas on Earth. It extends across all the countries that lie close to the North Pole, from Russia to Canada. In this region, it is very cold in the winter. That's why mostly conifers grow here. Brown bears feel at home in the cold taiga. With their thick brown fur, they are always nice and warm!

Elk live among the trees of the taiga. They are good swimmers and like to eat young conifers and bushes.

Which beaver can gnaw best?

THE AMAZONIAN RAINFOREST

The Amazonian rainforest is the largest rainforest in the world. This tropical rainforest follows the great Amazon River, which flows through nine countries. Sometimes the river is wide and quiet; elsewhere the Amazon is narrow and clatters like a waterfall. Lots of tall palm trees and other tropical plants grow on either side of the Amazon River. It's easy to get lost in this tropical forest!

Crocodiles and piranhas swim in the Amazon. Piranhas are carnivorous fish with sharp teeth. Yikes! So you'd better not go swimming in the Amazon!

Which inhabitants of the Amazon are dangerous?

THE FOREST TEMPLES OF ANGKOR

There are many temples in Angkor, Cambodia. They are very old and are found in the middle of a large forest. The trees of this forest have slowly grown over the temples. They started out next to the temples, then grew a little closer, and finally the trees started climbing all over the temples. Pretty, isn't it? The ancient trees of Angkor are famous around the world!

How many roots do you count?

CALGARY PUBLIC LIBRARY

P9-EJT-422

Henry Holt and Company, *Publishers since 1866*
Henry Holt® is a registered trademark of Macmillan Publishing Group, LLC
175 Fifth Avenue, New York, NY 10010 · mackids.com

Copyright © 2018 by Michael Slack. All rights reserved.

Library of Congress Cataloging-in-Publication Data is available.
ISBN 978-1-62779-270-7

Our books may be purchased in bulk for promotional, educational, or
business use. Please contact your local bookseller or the Macmillan Corporate
and Premium Sales Department at (800) 221-7945 ext. 5442 or
by e-mail at MacmillanSpecialMarkets@macmillan.com.

First edition, 2018 / Designed by April Ward and Sophie Erb
The illustrations for this book were digitally painted and collaged in Adobe Photoshop.
Printed in China by Toppan Leefung Printing Ltd., Dongguan City, Guangdong Province
1 3 5 7 9 10 8 6 4 2

For Tony Webb,
builder extraordinaire

BUNNY BUILT

MICHAEL SLACK

Christy Ottaviano Books

Henry Holt and Company · New York

LaRue was the handiest bunny in Westmore Oaks.

He had everything
an industrious bunny
could ever need.

Everything, that is,
except carrots.

He checked all of his usual hiding spots.

He was completely out.

So off he went to find some.

He stopped to ask Stella. "Do you have any carrots?"

"Afraid not. They were swept away when the wind blew down my house."

He stopped to ask Nevil. "Do you have any carrots?"
"Nope. They were in my boat but it sank."

He stopped to ask Ivy. "Do you have any carrots?"
"Sorry, LaRue. No carrots."
"What happened to your table?" Nevil asked Ivy.
"I gave it to Beaver. He needed wood to fix his dam.
But I found this beautiful rock to sit on."

"This is not a rock. It smells like carrots.
Maybe it's a seed," LaRue said.
Everyone chuckled. Everyone had an idea.
"You can have it, LaRue," said Ivy.

LaRue's friends helped him load the orange ball into his dump truck.

When he got home, LaRue went straight to work.

He **dug**.

He **dumped**.

He **dozed**.

He **doused**.

He waited.

Then he brought in
the heavy equipment.

The crane creaked.

Pulleys **pulled**.

The ground
shook and . . .

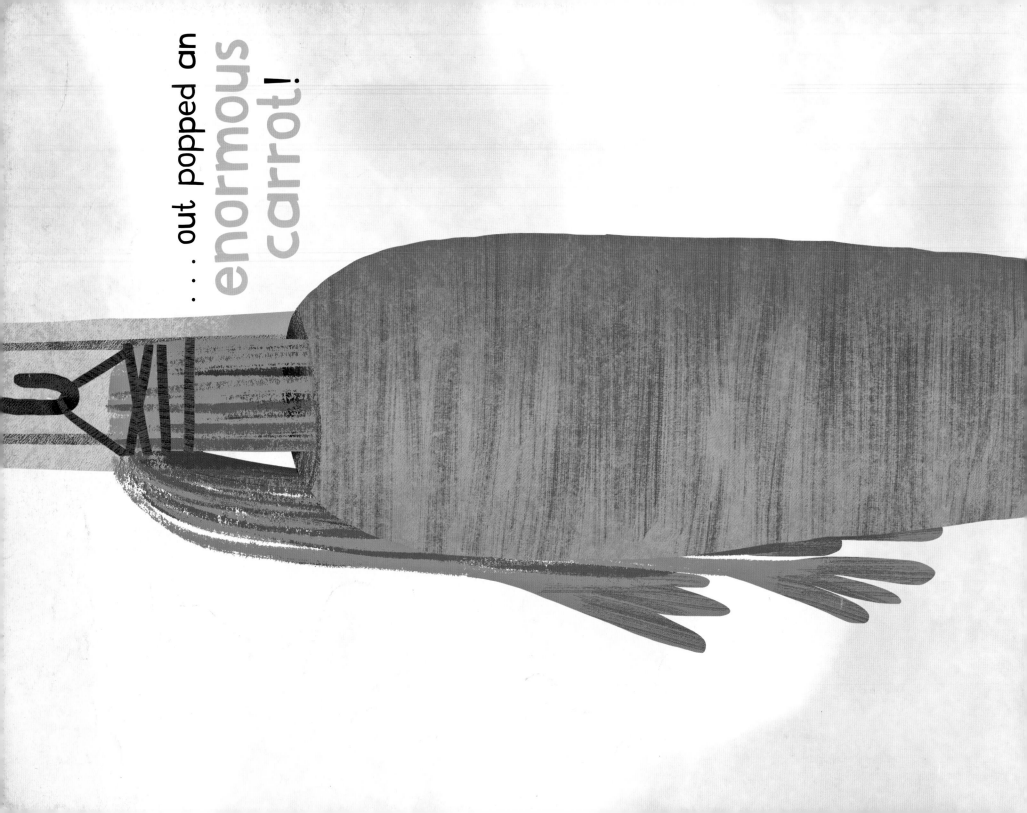

. . . out popped an **enormous carrot!**

"Whoa! What should I do with
all that carrot?" said LaRue.
Everyone had an idea.
But LaRue's idea was the best.

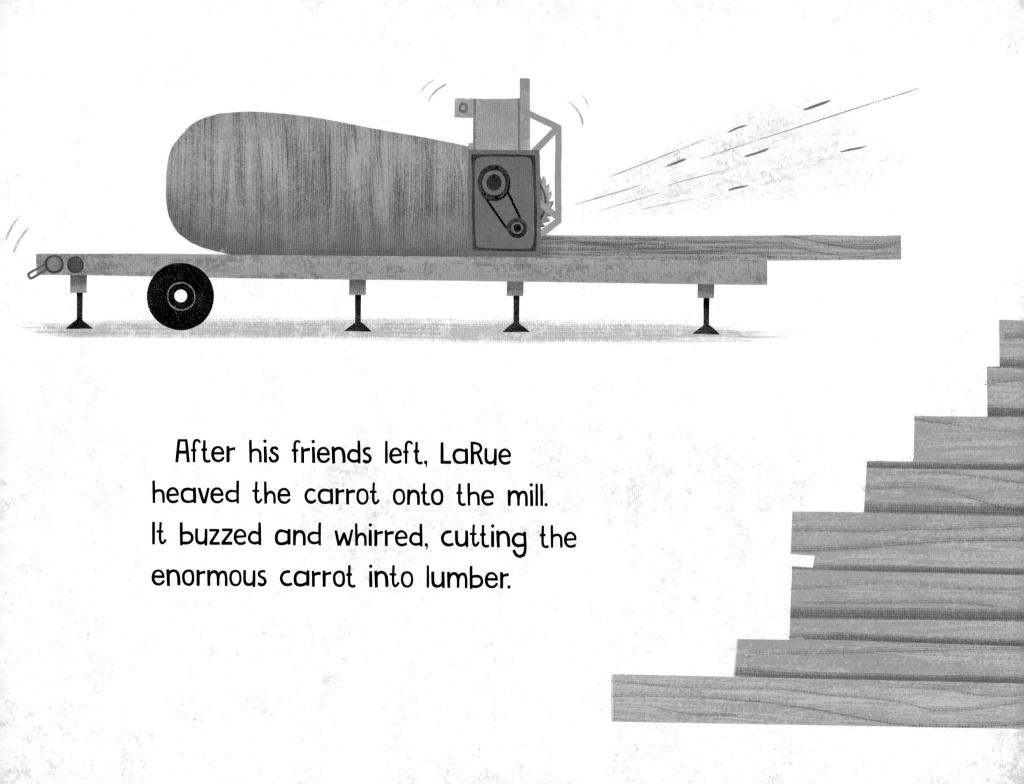

After his friends left, LaRue
heaved the carrot onto the mill.
It buzzed and whirred, cutting the
enormous carrot into lumber.

LaRue put on his tool belt and went straight to work.

First he built a house...

. . . then a boat

and last, a table.

He loaded them onto his big rig and off he went.

LaRue stopped to see **Ivy**

and **Nevil**

and Stella.

Then LaRue found a peaceful spot to eat the last tiny piece of the enormous carrot.

It tasted delicious!